Families are all unique and beautiful. Each family has it's own blend of people that are connected to each other.

All or some of your family will live with you at your home.

 Usually there will be other family members that live somewhere else. These folks can be called relatives. Some of us have lots of relatives while other people have few.

Families are all different. Your family may be bigger or smaller than your friends family, or other families that you know of. This is what makes family life interesting.

This is Carlie, she lives with her grandparents. She also gets to visit her mom quite often. Carlie loves being with her grandparents. They spend lots of time outside enjoying nature.

This is Michael. He lives with his 2 sisters and his mom and dad. They all live in the city but they love to visit the beach and go swimming in the summer.

This is Harjit's family. He lives with two sisters, a baby brother, his mom, dad and grandparents. This is a big family! They also have lots of family that visit from far away.

This is baby Liam and his mommy. This is his small family. Baby Liam's daddy passed away. His grandma does visit and help his mom out sometimes.

David has two daddies. Their names are Mark and Phillip. They love David very much. They spend lots of time going to the park, flying kites and playing sports together.

This is Damon and Natalie with their foster mom Koko. They live together but they also get to see their dad Jim and their stepmother Casey. They are part of their family too . Sometimes they all eat dinner together. They even go for visits to their Dad's house on weekends.

Tyson lives with his mom and his grandparents. His older cousin Terri also lives with them. Sometimes they get to see their aunties, uncles and other cousins on special occasions like Christmas or family birthdays.

This is Connie and Lena. They are a young married couple. They love each other but don't have any children yet. Not all families have children.

Mikayla lives with her brother Ozmund and her mom and dad. Ozmund uses a wheel chair to get around. Mikayla loves to play with Ozmund and go for walks to the shopping market. She is always willing to help her mommy with pushing the wheelchair.

Stephanie lives with her mom, step dad and her two twin step brothers Martin and Max. This is her family. Some people say this is a blended family but Stephanie just likes to be called a family. She also has a dad that she gets to visit every weekend.

This is Sam he lives with his mom and dad. Sam is adopted. Sam's parents really wanted a baby so they worked really hard to adopt Sam. This is their small family, but they do have grandparents and one auntie and uncle that live close by.

This is Annie and her baby brother Myles. Annie is a big sister and she loves it. She is really excited that her mommy Dianna and daddy Kyle are going to have another baby soon. They also have lots of aunties, uncles, cousins and grandparents that they visit with.

Families are all different but they have one thing in common. LOVE! Families love each other. That doesn't mean they don't sometimes disagree or argue but the family bond is always there.

Families are all connected through love.

What is your family like? Draw a picture of your family and write about it here.

_____

_____

_____

_____

Who are some of your relatives that are part of your family but don't live with you? You can draw their pictures here.

_____

_____

_____

_____

I love to have nice family dinners with my family. What are your favourite things to do with your family.

Thank you for reading "Family Life, Family Love." This book was created not only as a story but as a learning resource for young children. As an early childhood educator with over 25 years of experience in the field I wanted to fulfill my life long dream of getting many of my own written works published . I am hoping that this book helps children understand diversity that exists in families today and that many of them can see themselves and those they love in the illustrations.

Manufactured by Amazon.ca
Bolton, ON

29458263R10017